First Edition – 2025

Printed in the United States of America

No Fear In The Face Of Death

Preface:
Why I'm Not Afraid

There's a sacred silence in the room when someone takes their last breath. The kind of silence that feels like eternity paused for a moment to honor a soul passing through. I've stood in that silence more times than I can count. As a full-time hospice chaplain, I've walked families through heartbreak, held hands trembling with finality, and whispered prayers over fading pulses. And yet I'm not afraid of death.

I've seen it too closely, too often, and too personally to fear it.

You learn something after thousands of hours beside the dying: you learn what matters. You learn what fades. You learn what people cling to when everything else is slipping away. And most of all, you learn that death isn't the end it's the doorway.

I haven't just ministered to patients I've been ministered to by them. I've sat with atheists who asked me to pray "just in case," and with believers who saw angels before their eyes closed. I've watched family members forgive one another over hospice beds, and I've seen people wrestle with regrets they carried too long. In every encounter, I saw glimpses of the next world breaking through the veil of this one.

This book isn't just theology it's testimony. Not a theory about dying well, but a witness to what I've seen, felt, and held. I've watched the faith of saints shine brighter in their last days than in all the decades before. I've seen people slip into peace, not because they were perfect, but because they were prepared. They knew who held their tomorrow, so they didn't have to fear their today. There's a scripture that anchors me: "O death, where is thy sting? O grave, where is thy victory?" (1 Corinthians 15:55). That's not a poetic line it's a declaration. Death has no power over me, because I know the One who conquered it. I've seen the fear in the eyes of those who didn't know. And I've seen the calm in the faces of those who did.

So let me be honest with you I'm not writing this to impress you. I'm writing to prepare you. Not for dying, but for living living with the confidence that this world is not all there is. I want you to see what I've seen, feel what I've felt, and stand at the edge of this life not with dread, but with bold assurance.

I am not afraid.

Because I've stood beside death and seen Heaven wink.

Because I've heard the whispers of the soul saying, "I'm going home."

Because I've seen peace walk into a room when medicine had no more to offer.

Because I know without a doubt what comes next.

And by the time you finish this book I pray you will too.

Scott L. Gordon

Hospice Chaplain | Pastor | Witness

About the Author

Scott L. Gordon is a full-time hospice chaplain, senior pastor, and real estate entrepreneur who has walked faithfully beside the living and the dying for over two decades. With deep compassion and spiritual wisdom, he has held the hands of those taking their final breath and spoken peace into rooms where fear once ruled.

From hospital beds to pulpit platforms, Scott's life work has been rooted in faith, service, and truth. As a pastor for more than 25 years, he's preached the gospel with power and authenticity. As a chaplain, he's helped families find comfort when medical hope was gone. And as a man of deep conviction, he's lived what he teaches that death is not the end, but a doorway to something greater.

Scott is also the founder of a real estate business built on integrity, legacy, and impact. He uses his voice to mentor men, empower communities, and point others to Christ with clarity and compassion.

He resides in Oklahoma with his wife and family, continually serving with one mission in mind: to help people live fully and leave fearlessly.

Table of Contents

Chapter 1:
When the Room
Grows Still

There's a moment in almost every hospice room when everything goes quiet not just physically, but spiritually. The machines still hum, the family might whisper, but there's a silence that feels sacred. It's in that moment you realize: something bigger is happening. Something eternal.

I've been walking into rooms like that for over 20 years. Each one different, yet somehow the same. They all carry a weight, a sense of crossing. I've come to believe that when someone is about to leave this world, heaven leans in. And if you're still enough if you've learned to pay attention you can feel it.

I remember one of my very first patients Mr. Harold, a former school principal with a booming voice and a presence that used to command a room. But cancer had taken his strength. When I walked in that day, he was just a shadow of the man he used to be. Still, when he saw me, he smiled. I asked if I could pray with him. He said yes, and then he grabbed my hand and said, "Chaplain, I'm not scared. I know Who I belong to."

That stayed with me. It wasn't just what he said it was the peace in his eyes. The kind of peace you can't fake. He passed two days later. And when he did, his wife told me he just whispered, "I'm ready," and closed his eyes. That was it. No panic. No fear. Just peace.

Over the years, I've sat with hundreds of patients like Mr. Harold. Some believers. Some not. Some surrounded by family. Others completely alone. But the pattern never fails the room always grows still. And what happens in that stillness is where faith becomes sight.

I've heard things that can't be explained. I've seen people reach toward something invisible. I've watched smiles break across faces seconds before they took their final breath. One woman Miss Brown said, they're here, right before she passed. "Who's here?" I asked. She pointed to the corner and said, "The angels."

I don't tell these stories to sensationalize anything. I tell them because they're real. And because they've changed me. I used to think faith was something we used to get through life. But now I know it's also what carries us into eternity.

There was one night I'll never forget. A young man, only 38, dying from a rare disease. His wife had gone home to get some rest. He was alone when I arrived. He looked at me with tear-filled eyes and said, "Will it hurt?"

That question broke me. Not because I didn't have an answer, but because I knew what he was really asking: "Will it be, okay?"

I sat down, took his hand, and said, "I don't believe death hurts for those who know Jesus. I think it's like falling asleep in one world and waking up in another fully whole, fully healed, and finally home."
He nodded. We prayed. Two hours later, he passed

peacefully, quietly, with a small smile still on his face. That's what this chapter is about. The holy hush that comes before heaven. The stillness that testifies louder than any sermon I've ever preached.

I've preached hundreds of funerals. And while I've stood behind many pulpits, some of the most powerful sermons I've ever heard came from the deathbeds of people who never stood behind a mic. Their lives, their faith, and their deaths those were sermons I'll never forget.
When the room grows still, the noise of this life fades. The worries, the regrets, the questions they all settle. And what remains is what matters most: peace with God.

That's why I'm not afraid. I've seen too much. I've felt the brush of heaven in those quiet rooms. And I've come to believe, with everything in me, that death is not the end it's just the door.

So if you've ever wondered what happens when the time comes, let me assure you: if you know the One who holds eternity, you don't have to be afraid when the room grows still.

You just have to listen.

Chapter 2:
The People Who Died Well

There's a unique kind of peace I've come to recognize over the years. It's not something you can teach or manufacture it's something that only comes from knowing where you're going. I've seen it in the eyes of people who were just hours away from leaving this world. They weren't clinging to breath; they were resting in promises. These are the people who died well.

I'll never forget Miss Thelma. She was 91 years old, sharp as a tack, and full of joy, even as cancer ravaged her body. When I walked into her room for the first time, she greeted me with a smile and said, "Chaplain, I've been waiting on you. I knew you were coming." I smiled back and asked her what made her so sure. She said, "Because

I asked the Lord to send me someone who believed heaven is real and you look like you believe it."

That was the start of something special. Every visit with Miss Thelma turned into a worship session. She'd sing old hymns softly from her bed, hands lifted as far as they could go. She didn't fear death. In fact, she called it "going home."

"I've lived a good life, baby," she told me. "I've seen hard days, buried two children, survived a war, and prayed for more people than I can count. But now, I'm ready to see the One I've been singing about all these years."

Miss Thelma passed in her sleep one Sunday morning just as her family was singing "Great Is Thy Faithfulness" at her bedside. She died well. Then there was Deacon James. A tall man with a deep voice, once a strong leader in his church. ALS had taken away his ability to speak, but it hadn't touched his faith. I remember kneeling beside him as he tried to mouth words to me. He couldn't form them, but I knew what he was trying to say: "It is well." His wife leaned in and whispered, "He's been writing that down all week. That's the only thing he's been trying to tell people." When Deacon James died, it wasn't with bitterness it was with that same spirit. It was well with his soul. These are just two of many. I've seen former pastors, humble grandmothers, young mothers, and even teenagers face death with unshakable assurance not because they were fearless by nature, but because they had faith in something beyond this life. I think about a young girl named Mya only seventeen diagnosed with an aggressive cancer. In our first meeting, she asked me, "Do you think God made a mistake?" I sat with her, thinking carefully, and said, "I don't believe God makes mistakes. But I do believe He trusts you with something most of us will never understand." Over time, Mya became a light to everyone in the hospice. Nurses would stop by just to talk to her. She began writing notes of encouragement to other patients. Her body got weaker, but her spirit never dimmed. The day before she passed, she looked at me and said, "Tell them not to be sad. Tell them I'll be okay."

And she was. She passed holding her mother's hand, whispering the name of Jesus. There's something beautiful about dying well. It doesn't mean there's no pain, no tears, no sadness. It means there's a greater peace that surrounds the soul a peace that comes from relationship, not religion. When you know Jesus, death becomes a transition, not a termination.

One of the things I often share with families is this: dying well isn't about the condition of the body it's about the condition of the heart. I've seen people with terminal diagnoses live out their final days in worship, laughter, even gratitude. Not because their situation was easy but because their hearts were anchored. Sometimes people ask me, "How can you do this work every day? Doesn't it weigh on you?" The truth is, it does. There are moments when grief hits me in waves. But then I think about the ones who died well. I remember the strength in their silence, the conviction in their eyes, and the joy that lingered in the room after they were gone. That's what keeps me going. They remind me of Paul's words: "I have fought the good fight, I have finished the race, I have kept the faith."

This chapter isn't just about those who passed it's about those who taught me how to live. Because when you see someone die well, it changes how you face life. You begin to ask better questions: Am I ready? What legacy am I leaving? Who am I trusting in the end? The people who died well didn't just teach me how to be a better chaplain they taught me how to be a better man. A better pastor. A better believer. And I pray, when my time comes, that I will face it the same way they did hand in hand with Jesus, eyes set on eternity, and heart full of peace. Because that's what dying well really is. It's knowing where you're going and Who's waiting for you when you get there.

Chapter 3:
The People Who Died Afraid

This chapter is the hardest for me to write. Not because I don't know what to say, but because these stories still sit heavy in my heart. As a hospice chaplain, I've had the sacred honor of walking with many people to the edge of eternity. But not every journey end in peace. Some people die afraid. Their faces stay with me the way their eyes darted around the room, the way their hands trembled, the way they whispered questions that should've been answered long before their final hours. I've seen people cry out for help, not because of pain, but because of panic. Panic that comes when you're not sure what's waiting on the other side. There was a man named Walter. He was 67, a retired truck driver. We didn't meet until the final week of his life. I remember walking into his room for the first time he looked at me and said, "Preacher, I need you to tell me it's gonna be okay." I paused and sat down beside him. "Do you believe in Jesus?" I asked. He looked away. "I did once. But I got too far gone." That broke my heart. Walter had spent most of his adult life angry angry at God, angry at the church, angry at himself. His wife had died of cancer twenty years earlier, and he never forgave God for it. He told me he stopped praying the day she died. In our final visits, we talked a lot. He cried more than he talked. He said, "I'm scared, Chaplain. What if He doesn't take me?" I did my best to assure him that grace doesn't expire. That God's mercy reaches even into hospital rooms. We prayed together. I believe God met him in that place. But the fear never fully left his face. Walter's story isn't unique. Over the years, I've met many like him people who ran from God, ignored Him, rejected Him and now, at the end, weren't sure where they stood. There was a woman named Judy. She was well off, successful, owned several properties, and had three grown children. But in the end, none of that mattered. She had built a life full of things but not faith. And when her time came, she wasn't ready. She told me; I've always controlled everything. My business, my money, even my kids. But I can't control this. And that terrifies me. Judy had never really thought about death until her diagnosis. And by then, she told me it felt too late. We had deep conversations in her final days. She admitted she didn't know how to let go. She didn't know how to trust anyone let alone God. There's a fear that comes with dying when you've never truly lived with purpose. A fear that whispers, "Did I miss it?" I've seen that fear in the eyes of many. And while I believe God is merciful, I also believe these stories should serve as a wake-up call not just to the dying, but to the living. Death is not the time to start asking eternal questions. The most painful part of these moments is knowing peace was possible faith was available but it was pushed aside, traded for success, distractions, or bitterness. I remember one man Ronald who said to me, "I thought I had more time." That's the line I've heard the most from those who die afraid. "I thought I had more time." But none of us knows how much time we have. And that's why I plead with people every chance I get don't wait until the end to get things right with God. Some people say, "I'll get saved when I'm older," or, "I'm not ready yet." But the truth is none of us are guaranteed tomorrow. And the worst thing in the world is to come to the edge

21

of eternity unsure of where you stand. These stories are hard, but they're necessary. I share them not to scare you, but to remind you peace doesn't come automatically. It's found in relationship with the One who conquered death. I've watched people try to make peace with the past in their final hours. Some did. Some didn't. But every single one of them wished they had started sooner. So, if you're reading this and you've been running stop. If you've been pushing God away turn around. If you've been living like you've got forever remember, you don't. The people who died afraid taught me that regret is a heavy thing to carry into eternity. But they also taught me something else: as long as there's breath, there's still hope. Even in the final hours, God can meet you. Even in the last breath, His mercy can reach you. But don't wait for the stillness of the room to seek the peace of heaven. Seek Him now. Because no one should die afraid.

Chapter 4:
The Family That Let
Go Too Soon

Death doesn't just affect the one passing it reaches everyone in the room. As a hospice chaplain, I've seen death draw families together in ways that are beautiful and healing. But I've also seen death become a wedge separating people emotionally long before the final breath is taken. Some families check out too soon. They let go before it's time. Not because they don't love their loved one, but because the pain is too great. It's a kind of emotional self-preservation distancing themselves in hopes of softening the blow. But in doing so, they miss sacred moments they'll never get back. I remember a man named Mr. Lee. A proud Army veteran in his eighties. Strong-willed, stern, but deeply respectful. He was dying from congestive heart failure. His daughter, Teresa, visited often but over time, her visits grew shorter and more spaced out. One day, she said to me, "It's too hard. I can't stand to see him like this." I understood her pain. Watching someone you love fade is gut-wrenching. But I also knew something she didn't yet realize: presence matters more than comfort. Mr. Lee asked about her every day. "Did Teresa come by?" he'd ask, eyes scanning the door. I'd tell him yes, or no, or "She said she'll try tomorrow." And every time, he'd nod quietly, hiding his disappointment.

When he passed, Teresa was across town. She arrived an hour too late. Through tears, she told me, "I thought I had more time. I didn't think it would happen today." But the truth is, her absence had started long before that. She let go too soon not physically, but emotionally. I've seen it happen in many families. Sometimes it's the adult children who can't bear to watch the decline. Sometimes it's a spouse who begins grieving early and mentally steps away, trying to protect their heart.

But here's the hard truth: letting go too soon robs both sides.

The dying need our presence. Even when they can't respond. Even when they're unconscious. There's power in simply being there holding their hand, speaking their name, reading scripture, singing softly. I've seen patients unresponsive for days suddenly react when a loved one enters the room. I've watched heart rates change, tears form, or muscles relax just because someone they loved spoke to them. Presence is ministry. There was a woman named Gloria who was dying from a rare neurological disease. She couldn't speak or move much, but her husband came every day. He would sit next to her and read their love letters from the 1970s. Every single day. One nurse asked him, "Do you think she can hear you?" He replied, "I don't know. But I want her to feel love all the way to the end." That's the kind of presence that brings peace.

Gloria passed with him at her side, reading the final line of a letter that said, "You will always be my home." Too often, I've seen families withdraw because they don't know what to say. But the truth is you don't have to say anything. Your presence is enough. If you've ever walked this road if you've ever lost someone and now carry the weight of stepping away too soon, I want to tell you something: grace covers even that. This chapter isn't about guilt it's about awareness. To those who are walking with someone through the valley of the shadow of death: stay close. Lean in, even when it's hard. Cry with them. Pray with them. Sit in the silence with them. Because when it's over, what you'll remember isn't the tubes or the diagnosis you'll remember the sacredness of those final moments. You'll remember the peace in their eyes. You'll remember the chance to say, "I love you," one last time. And they'll remember you were there. As much as we try to protect ourselves from pain, we were made for presence. That's how Jesus showed His love by showing up. By drawing near. Even in death. So let this chapter be a reminder: don't check out too soon. Stay until the very end. Because sometimes, the greatest healing happens in the final goodbye.

Chapter 5: The Family That Wouldn't Let Go

Love is powerful. It can bind us together, heal wounds, and carry us through storms. But when it comes to death, even love must learn when to release. In my years as a hospice chaplain, I've walked with families through all kinds of grief. Some let go too soon but others, out of deep love and desperation, hold on so tightly that they prolong the pain. This chapter is about those families. The ones who couldn't let go. The ones who weren't ready even when the patient was. I remember a woman named Margaret. She had lived a full life ninety-three years, five children, dozens of grandchildren. Her faith was solid, and her heart was at peace. Every time I visited, she would say, "I'm ready. I've talked to God.

I've made peace." But her daughter, Elaine, wasn't ready. Elaine was her youngest, the caregiver, the one who had stayed. She had given up her job, her social life, and almost everything to take care of her mother. In many ways, Margaret had become her whole world. So, when Margaret's health began to fail, Elaine resisted every step. She questioned the doctors, refused to sign hospice papers at first, and asked me over and over, "Do you think there's still a chance?" I could hear the fear in her voice the fear of losing her mother, but also the fear of losing her identity. The day before Margaret passed, I sat with them both. Margaret could barely speak, but she whispered to me, "I'm trying to go but she won't let me." That moment almost broke me. Sometimes, our refusal to release is not about the other person it's about us. Our fear. Our pain. Our need. Elaine loved her mother deeply. But her clinging turned into resistance. And that resistance made the transition harder for both of them. When Margaret passed, Elaine fell apart. Not just from grief, but from regret. "I should've let her go," she said, sobbing. "I held on too tight."

I didn't rebuke her. I simply held her hand and said, you loved her the best you knew how. Still, her story stays with me. There was another family who kept insisting on more treatments, even when the patient was ready to rest. The man Henry was exhausted. His body was shutting down. But his sons kept asking doctors to "try one more thing." They brought in specialists. They pushed back on comfort care. When I asked Henry how he felt, he said, "I just want peace. But I don't want to disappoint them." That's the kind of pressure some patients carry wanting to please their families, even in death. Letting go is never easy. It's one of the hardest acts of love. But it's also one of the holiest. It doesn't mean giving up. It means trusting that God's plan includes rest. That death is not defeat, but a divine transition. I've sat in rooms where the only thing standing between peace and passing was the family's refusal to release. I've seen patients linger for days, almost as if they were waiting for permission to go. And I've seen what happens when that permission is finally given. There was a man named Charles, whose wife hadn't spoken to him in years due to a family rift. But when she heard he was dying, she came. She walked into the room, took his hand, and said, "Charles, I forgive you. You can go now." He passed within minutes. Sometimes, closure is the key. Families often struggle with guilt. They think letting go means they don't love enough. But it's the opposite. Letting go, when it's time, is one of the deepest expressions of love. It says, "I love you enough to release you. I love you enough to trust God with you." If you're reading this and you're holding on search your heart. Are you holding on for them or for you? Love them enough to listen. Watch their body. Hear their spirit. Ask God for the courage to say what they need to hear: "It's okay. You can rest now." I've watched that sentence unlock peace. And afterward, I've heard families say, "It was the most beautiful moment of my life." Because when you let go, you give space for the holy. You create room for peace. You surrender control and receive grace. The family that wouldn't let go taught me something important: love doesn't cling, it releases. And when it's time to say goodbye, the most loving thing you can do is let them go home.

Chapter 6:
When a Child Dies

There's no way to prepare for the death of a child. Even in my role as a hospice chaplain where most of my work has been with adults, I've seen the ripple effect when a young life is cut short. Most of the time, it doesn't happen in a hospital bed surrounded by equipment but rather through the stories people carry into the rooms I serve. I've ministered to grandparents who were broken over a grandchild taken too soon. I've sat with mothers and fathers who, while facing their own mortality, still grieved a son or daughter lost decades earlier. The grief never fully goes away it just finds a place to live. There was a patient named Mr. Donald who was dying of advanced cancer. In one of our deeper conversations, he told me, "I buried my son at nineteen. Car accident. It never leaves you." His eyes welled up as he talked. "That pain, Chaplain it's the kind that goes with you everywhere. I've lived a good life, but that piece of me it's still out there." He pulled out a worn photo from his wallet. The edges were faded, but the love was still sharp. "I used to talk to him in my sleep," he said. "And now that I'm leaving, I just hope I hope I'll see him again." We sat quietly for a while. Then I told him what I tell every grieving parent: "God holds our children. And the hope of heaven is not just for comfort it's for reunion." That moment reminded me that while my ministry centers on the dying, it also ministers to the losses people carry with them to their own graves. Grief over a child can be silent. Deep. Generational. I've had patients who never spoke about it until the end. One woman, Miss Charlene, told me about the daughter she lost at birth. It had been over fifty years. But as she spoke, her voice cracked like it had just happened. I never really mourned," she said. "I just got up the next day and went on with life." She asked me to pray with her not for her sickness, but for the healing of that old wound. And that's what I've learned: even in hospice, we're not just dealing with the present we're touching the past. People don't just die from illness.

They carry emotional scars, regrets, and silent grief all the way to their final breath. Sometimes, the greatest peace comes not from pain management, but from heart release. So, this chapter is not about pediatric hospice. It's about the unspoken grief so many adults carry the child they lost, the guilt they buried, the questions they never answered.

And it's about God's mercy for all of it. To the father who wonders if he could've done more to the mother who carries shame for things beyond her control to the grandparent who never got to say goodbye hear me when I say: God sees. God knows. And God heals even that. Heaven is not just a place of peace it's a place of restoration. I've prayed with fathers who said, "I just want to hold them again." And I believe with all my heart they will. We may not have all the answers here. But we serve a God who promises there will be no more death, no more crying, and no more pain. That promise includes every loss we've endured even the ones we never talk about. So, if you've lost a child, in any way, at any age this chapter is for you. You're not forgotten. Your grief is valid. And your healing is possible. God hasn't forgotten your pain. And He certainly hasn't forgotten your child.

Chapter 7: I've Seen Heaven in Their Eyes

There's something sacred about the final moments of life that no textbook can prepare you for. I've seen things in those quiet hours that theology couldn't teach me things that changed the way I see heaven, eternity, and the thin space between here and glory. I've seen heaven in their eyes. It's not always dramatic. It's often subtle a shift in the atmosphere, a change in their breath, or the way their gaze locks onto something just beyond the room. But when it happens, you know. It's not fear. It's not confusion. It's wonder. One of my patients, Mr. Calvin, had battled illness for years. He was quiet, reserved, a man of faith but not one to talk much about heaven. On his final day, he opened his eyes, looked over my shoulder, and began to smile. He whispered, "I see them." I asked gently, "Who do you see, Mr. Calvin?" He said,

"My brothers. And my mama. Lord, they look good."
And then he slipped into eternity. I've seen this time
and again. Patients who hadn't spoken in days suddenly
become alert. Their eyes scan the ceiling or the corner of
the room, and a peace wash over them. It's as if heaven
opens just enough for them to see who's waiting. One
woman, Miss Roberta, was near the end. Her breathing
was shallow, and her family was gathered, quietly
praying. Suddenly, she sat up halfway, looked to the side,
and whispered, "Jesus. You came." Tears fell down her
cheeks as she laid back down and passed within minutes.
Her daughter looked at me and said, "She wasn't alone."
No, she wasn't.

There's a passage in Acts 7 that tells of Stephen, the first
Christian martyr. As he was being stoned, Scripture says
he looked up and saw Jesus standing at the right hand of
God. Not sitting standing. It's the only time in the Bible
where Jesus is depicted as standing in heaven. I believe
that's what happens when saints go home. I believe
heaven stands to welcome them. I've seen patients reach
their arms up as if being lifted. I've heard people say,
"The light is so bright," or, "He's here." And every time, I

stand still because I know I'm on holy ground. These moments don't just comfort the dying they minister to the living. I've watched families cry tears of joy in the middle of loss because they knew their loved one saw heaven before they left. It reminds me that heaven isn't a distant hope it's a present reality breaking through at just the right time. And sometimes, that glimpse is all we need to carry us through grief. Not every patient sees visions or speaks final words. But for those who do, it's like a curtain is pulled back for just a moment. And in that moment, eternity feels close. I've learned to pay attention to their eyes. Eyes that once held fear now soften. Eyes that were dim now brighten. And in those eyes, I've seen something greater than what this world can offer. I've seen faith becoming sight. There was a man named Gerald who had always struggled with belief. He grew up in church but walked away in his twenties. On his final day, after hours of labored breathing, he opened his eyes wide and whispered, "I didn't think it would be like this." I leaned in. "What do you see?" He smiled and said, "Peace. So much peace." Then he passed. That single sentence undid me. These stories aren't fiction. They are testimony reminders that our faith is not in vain. That heaven is not a metaphor. That we are heading somewhere real.

When I say I've seen heaven in their eyes, I mean it. Not just light or color but something deeper. A knowing. A recognition. A homecoming. And every time I witness it, my own faith grows stronger. My own fear shrinks smaller. Because if heaven is this real at the edge of life, then how glorious must it be on the other side? So, I'll keep standing in those rooms. I'll keep watching those eyes. I'll keep whispering prayers as eternity draws near. And when my time comes, I'll look toward that same corner expecting to see the One I've preached about, sang to, and trusted for a lifetime. Because I've seen heaven. And I know it's waiting

Chapter 8:
Death Is Not the End

In a world that fears death, I've come to see it differently not as a conclusion, but as a transition. As a hospice chaplain for over two decades, I've walked with people to the edge of this life more times than I can count. And with every step, I've become more convinced of one truth: Death is not the end. It might feel like an end. To the families left behind, it often looks final. The closing of a chapter. The end of a voice, a laugh, a presence that once filled the room. But when you've been in as many rooms as I have when you've stood beside believers in their final moments you begin to understand something deeper. Death isn't a wall. It's a doorway.I remember a man named Brother Amos. He was a deacon at his church for over forty years. The cancer had spread throughout his body, and the doctors said he didn't have long. When I walked into his room that day, he looked at me and said, "Chaplain I'm not dying I'm transitioning." I smiled. "You're right." He chuckled and said, "I've preached about heaven too long to be scared of it now. I'm finally going to see what I've been shouting about." And he did. With his family surrounding him, he raised one hand in the air and whispered, "Glory," before taking his final breath. That's not the end. In John 11, Jesus arrives at the tomb of Lazarus after his friend has already been dead for four days. Everyone around Him is mourning, weeping, wailing. But Jesus says something powerful: "I am the resurrection and the life. He who believes in Me, though he may die, he shall live."

That's the foundation of our hope. Not that we'll live forever in this body but that death is not the final word. Time and time again, I've watched people face their final hours with peace not because they were pain-free, but because they knew this was not the end of their story. Faith teaches us that death has been defeated. The cross settled that. The resurrection proved it. So, when I say "death is not the end," I'm not offering a poetic sentiment. I'm declaring a spiritual reality. I've seen it in the way a room fills with peace after a believer passes. I've felt it in the prayers of families who know their loved one is now home. I've seen it in the strength of those left behind, knowing they will see them again. One of my patients, a woman named Linda, said something I'll never forget. She was weeks from passing, but fully alert and aware. She said, "Chaplain, I'm going to graduate soon. I'm just waiting on my name to be called." That image stuck with me graduation. Moving from one level to another. It's not a loss. It's a promotion. Sometimes people ask me, "How do you stay strong doing this kind of work?" And I tell them it's because I've seen the other side. Maybe not with my eyes, but through the eyes of those who've crossed over. I've felt the assurance in their final words. I've heard the stories of visions, songs, light, and peace. And I've read the Scriptures that confirm what my heart already believes. Paul said, "To be absent from the body is to be present with the Lord." Not might be. Not someday. But present. Immediately. That's our hope.

So I live with a kind of urgency, but not fear. I want people to know that death is not something to be feared it's something to prepare for. Because how we live now shapes how we'll leave.

I want to encourage you today: if you're facing death, or if someone you love is, hold tight to this truth this life is not all there is. We were made for more. And for those in Christ, what comes next is more glorious than anything we've ever known.

So no, this is not the end. It's only the beginning.

Chapter 9: When God Tells You to Just Sit

Not every moment at the bedside is filled with words. In fact, some of the most powerful moments in hospice have been completely silent. As a chaplain, I used to think I had to always say something offer a verse, a prayer, a comforting phrase. But over time, I learned that some of the most sacred ministry happens when I simply sit. There was a man named Larry, a former construction worker with calloused hands and a gruff voice. He wasn't much of a talker. His illness had stolen his strength, and his family had already said their goodbyes. When I entered his room, I introduced myself, but he didn't respond. He just looked at me tired, worn, but aware. I pulled up a chair, sat beside him, and said, "I'm here, brother. Just here." For the next forty-five minutes, neither of us said a word. He didn't ask for prayer. I didn't quote Scripture. I just sat. And as I sat, I felt peace. When his daughter came in, she found us like that. She whispered, "Thank you. He doesn't like a lot of noise. But he doesn't like to be alone either." That moment taught me something I've never forgotten: presence is powerful. Sometimes, God doesn't call you to preach. He calls you to be still. To sit with someone in their final moments and let your presence say what your words cannot. There have been times I've walked into rooms where families are emotionally exhausted. They've cried, prayed, begged and now, they're empty. What they need isn't more activity. They need peace.

And peace rarely shouts.

I've sat in living rooms with the television off and the air thick with grief. I've sat in hospital corners as machines beeped and nurses moved around quietly. I've sat with people whose loved ones were transitioning, and all they wanted was someone to be with them. Jesus modeled this. In the Garden of Gethsemane, He asked His disciples to simply sit and pray with Him. He didn't ask them to perform, preach, or fix anything just to stay near. The ministry of presence. And later, when Martha was busy serving and Mary was at Jesus' feet, Jesus affirmed Mary not for doing, but for sitting. There is a holiness in stillness.

I remember a woman named Mrs. Evelyn. She had been on hospice for months. Her decline was slow, but steady. One afternoon, her family had to step away. I volunteered to sit with her. She slept most of the time, but every now and then, she'd open her eyes just enough to see I was still there. That was enough. Her breathing slowed, her body calmed, and eventually she slipped into eternity as I held her hand. No words. No sermon. Just presence. I've learned that when God tells you to just sit, it's not a dismissal it's an invitation. An invitation to step into sacred space, to hold space for someone else, to carry peace into a storm without saying a word. For those walking with the dying, know this: your silence can be healing. Your stillness can be strength. You don't have to have answers. You don't need the perfect thing to say. Sometimes, the most Christ-like thing you can do is sit. Sit with the hurting. Sit with the doubting. Sit with the afraid. Not to fix them, but to be with them. When God tells you to just sit, obey. Because in that sitting, heaven often draws near. Peace settles in. Fear begins to lift. And souls prepare for flight. You don't need to fill the air with words. You just need to bring His presence into the room. So, sit. And let God do what only He can do.

Chapter 10:
What I Told My Own
Family

After all the hospital rooms I've walked into, all the hands I've held, and all the final breaths I've witnessed, there's one group of people I've never stopped thinking about my own family. You can't do this kind of work and not reflect on your own mortality. Every time I leave a patient's bedside, I'm reminded that one day, someone will sit at mine. And when that time comes, I want my family to know exactly where I stand. I want them to know what I believe, what I hope for, and what I've tried to live. So, I've told them. I've told my children, my wife, and those closest to me that I'm not afraid of death. Not because I'm brave, but because, I'm sure. Sure, of God's promises. Sure, of His grace. Sure, of heaven. I've told them, "Don't fight for me to stay if God is calling me home. Let me go. Rejoice in the life I lived. Grieve but don't despair. Because I'll be more alive in that moment than I've ever been." We don't talk about these things enough. We avoid the topic; afraid it will make things too real. But death is real. And preparation is love. I've sat with too many families who didn't know what their loved one believed. They didn't know if they wanted prayer, or worship, or scripture. They didn't know how to say goodbye because the conversations never happened. I never wanted that for my family. So, I've talked to them. Not in fear but in faith. I've told them what songs I'd want played at my service. I've shared the scriptures that carried me through storms. I've made peace with my past so they won't have to untangle it later. I told my son one day, "Don't let death be a thief. Let it be a testimony." I want my life to preach even after I'm gone. I want my children to remember not just what I said, but how I lived. I want my wife to have peace knowing I loved her fully. And I want my legacy to be one of faith, not fear. I've told my family, "You don't have to pretend to be strong. It's okay to cry. But don't let grief swallow you. Let it deepen you." Because that's what loss does when you anchor it in Christ it grows you. It opens your eyes to what matters. It makes every hug, every conversation,

every shared meal more precious. One of the greatest gifts we can give our families is clarity. Clarity about what we believe. Clarity about how we want to be remembered. Clarity about where we're going. So, I've tried to leave no confusion. I've written things down. I've had hard conversations. And I've lived my faith in front of them not perfectly, but persistently. Because when that day comes, I don't want them guessing. I want them to say, "Daddy told us this day would come. And he told us not to be afraid." If you haven't talked to your family about these things yet start. Don't wait for a diagnosis or a tragedy. Talk while you're healthy. Lead while you're strong. Tell them what you believe.
Tell them what you hope for. Tell them where your faith lies.

Because the day will come when your silence will speak for you. And what you've lived and said will be the message your family holds onto. As for me, I've told them everything they need to know. And most importantly, I've told them where to find me. Home.

Chapter 11:
How Heaven Changes Everything

I've seen a lot of things in over twenty years as a hospice chaplain grief, anger, joy, silence, surrender. But the one thing that changes the atmosphere more than anything else is hope. And for believers, that hope has a name. It's called heaven.

Heaven changes everything. I've watched rooms filled with sorrow suddenly transform when the reality of heaven becomes more real than the diagnosis. I've seen family members lift their heads, tears still fresh, but peace in their eyes, because they knew this is not the end. Heaven gives perspective. It reframes suffering. It doesn't take away the sting of death, but it strips death of its victory. There was a woman named Catherine. She was a schoolteacher, retired and living alone when she was diagnosed with a terminal illness. I visited her

49

regularly, and on one of my final visits, she looked at me and said, "Chaplain, I've been thinking about all the children I taught over the years and now I get to be taught something."

What do you mean?" I asked. She smiled. "I get to learn what heaven looks like. And I'm not afraid." Heaven had become more than a concept for her. It was a destination. She passed quietly, peacefully, with a Bible on her lap and a worship song playing on her little bedside radio. And in that room, there was no fear only peace. That's what heaven does. It quiets the panic. It answers the "why" with "wait and see." It reminds us that the grave is not a period it's a comma. The more I've thought about heaven, the more I've realized it doesn't just prepare us to die it changes how we live.

When you know that this life is not all there is, you begin to hold things differently. You stop chasing what doesn't matter. You forgive quicker. You love deeper. You become more present, more grateful, more rooted. Heaven makes us generous, because we're not clinging to things that

rust. Heaven makes us brave, because what can man do
to us if eternity is secure?

Heaven makes us focused, because we're not running
a race for a trophy that fades, we're pressing toward a
crown that lasts forever. Paul said in Philippians 1:21,
"For to me, to live is Christ, and to die is gain." That only
makes sense if you know something better is coming.
And we do. Jesus said He was going to prepare a place
for us. A real place. Not an idea, not a metaphor a
home. With no more tears, no more sickness, no more
goodbyes. I've preached about heaven. I've studied it.
I've taught on it. But more than that, I've seen it in the
way people pass with smiles, with songs, with hands
raised. I've seen it in the way families grieve with hope,
not despair. I've seen it in the way patients light up at
the thought of seeing Jesus' face to face. Heaven is not a
myth we cling to in weakness it's the truth that gives us
strength. I once asked a dying man if he was afraid. He
looked me in the eye and said, "Chaplain, I'm not afraid
of where I'm going. I'm just sorry to leave the ones I love.
But I'll see them again." That's the power of heaven. It
doesn't just give peace to the dying it gives purpose to

the living. So, I keep showing up. I keep praying. I keep holding hands and whispering scriptures. Because I know what's on the other side. And I want every person I meet to know it too. Heaven changes how we grieve. Heaven changes how we let go. Heaven changes how we hope. And yes, heaven changes everything.

Chapter 12:
For Anyone Who's Afraid Right Now

If you're reading this chapter, and your heart is gripped by fear, I want you to know something: You are not alone. I've walked into countless rooms over the years where fear was thick in the air. Not just the fear of dying but the fear of pain, the unknown, separation, and what comes next. I've seen it in the eyes of patients. I've seen it on the faces of family members. And yes, I've felt it myself. But what I've also seen and what I want to offer you right now is a peace that doesn't come from understanding everything, but from trusting the One who does.

This chapter is written for the person who doesn't know if they're ready. For the one who has questions that haven't been answered. For the one who's trying to be strong but feels overwhelmed. For the one who is afraid.

Let me speak to you not as a chaplain, not as a pastor but as someone who has sat in the presence of dying men and women and witnessed something greater than fear. I've seen fear melt away in the presence of love. I've seen panic silenced by a single verse. I've seen trembling hands grow still when reminded of heaven.

The fear you're feeling is real. But it's not final. God is not disappointed in you because you're afraid. He's not asking you to pretend to be brave. He's inviting you to trust Him in your weakness. Psalm 56:3 says, "When I am afraid, I put my trust in You." Not "if" but "when." God knew there would be moments when fear comes knocking. But He also gave us a response: trust. If you're afraid right now, I encourage you to pause and take a deep breath. Whisper this prayer: "God, I don't know what's coming, but I trust that You're already there." You don't have to walk this journey alone. You don't have to have all the answers. You don't even have to be fearless. You just need to know Who goes with you. Jesus said, "I will never leave you nor forsake you." That promise is for this moment. Right now. In the middle of the unknown.

I've seen people who started their hospice journey filled with fear and ended it filled with peace. Not because their circumstances changed, but because they surrendered their fear to a God who's bigger than death. If you've lost someone and are afraid of what your life will look like now, please hear me: you will survive this. God will carry you. And your pain does not disqualify you from peace. If you're facing your own mortality, please know: you are seen. You are loved. And you are not walking this valley alone.

Heaven is not a fairytale it's real. And it's closer than you think.
So take one step. Pray one prayer. Whisper one "yes" to God.

Because faith doesn't always roar. Sometimes, it looks like a scared soul still choosing to believe. I've sat with those who doubted, who wept, who wrestled and I've seen God meet them right where they were. He'll meet you too. Let this chapter be your reminder that fear doesn't have the final word. Faith does.
Peace does. Heaven does. And the same God who has

walked with me through hospital rooms, hospice beds, and final breaths is walking with you now. So, if you're afraid, that's okay.

Just don't stay afraid. Take God's hand. Let Him lead you home.

Final Charge: I Know What Comes Next

This isn't just a book it's a piece of my heart.

If you've made it this far, I want to thank you. Thank you for allowing me to walk with you through some of the most sacred moments I've witnessed. Thank you for letting me share stories, sorrows, and the deep hope I've found at the edge of life.

Everything I've written here comes from real rooms, real people, and real moments with God.

I've watched souls take flight.
I've watched peace flood rooms like sunlight through a window.

I've stood still when heaven came close, and I've knelt in silence as people crossed over into glory.

And through it all, I've come to believe one thing more than anything else:

I know what comes next.

Not because I've been there but because I've seen the evidence over and over again. Because the same God who held me through my storms has been faithful to every person I've walked with in theirs.

I've been in ministry for a long time. I've preached funerals. I've buried friends. I've comforted strangers. But nothing has shaped my faith more than hospice ministry. In those rooms, I found the power of presence} In those eyes, I saw glimpses of heaven. And in those final breaths, I heard whispers of eternity.
I want you to carry this truth with you: you don't have to be afraid. Whether you're standing by a loved one's bedside or facing your own diagnosis whether you're dealing with grief, fear, or just deep questions there is

a peace that surpasses understanding, and His name is Jesus. Heaven is not just a hope it's home. It's where there's no more cancer. No more regrets. No more tears. Just joy, reunion, and the fullness of God's love.

I wrote this book so you wouldn't't have to guess. So, you wouldn't't have to wonder. So, you could hear, through the voice of a chaplain who's seen too much to doubt it: Heaven is real. And God is faithful. So, here's my final charge: Live ready. Love deeply. Say what needs to be said. Hold the ones who matter close. And never let fear rob you of peace. Because when it's your time when the room grows still, and your breath slows, and you feel the nearness of eternity I want you to remember this: You are not alone. You are seen. You are held. You are known. And heaven is waiting. With all my heart,

Made in the USA
Monee, IL
24 September 2025